E. R. Landon

MAKING THE BRUSH
BEHAVE

"Rio Frias in the Andes"
by Eliot O'Hara

Making the Brush Behave

FOURTEEN LESSONS IN WATERCOLOR PAINTING
WITH TWENTY-NINE ILLUSTRATIONS

BY ELIOT O'HARA
AUTHOR OF "MAKING WATERCOLOR BEHAVE"

New York

MINTON, BALCH & COMPANY

Printed in the United States of America

To
Shirley Putnam O'Hara
who made the text behave

CONTENTS

8 CONTENTS

ILLUSTRATIONS

(Photographs by Juley, New York; and Woltz, Washington)

FOREWORD

THIS book presents in abridged form the method of teaching watercolor technique in the Eliot O'Hara School of Watercolor Painting, Goose Rocks Beach, Maine, as well as in my courses given in other parts of the country. It supplements, rather than replaces, my first book, "Making Watercolor Behave," written in 1932, and now in its fourth and revised printing. As nearly as is possible, through printed type and without demonstration, also without the advantage of questions by the student, it tells how certain effects may be obtained with the brush and colors.

The theory of its teaching is predicated on the assumption that art itself cannot be taught. If a student has good taste in color and an instinct for design he may hope to become a painter. If his taste is bad or he lacks inventiveness, if he is not observant and has no flair for balance and line, then he can only be taught rules and formulae and his work will be imitative and conventional. In either case the student *can* be taught the technical part of painting, just as a writer can build a vocabulary, or a musician learn the fingering of his instrument.

There are two opposing theories of teaching: the prevailing one instructs the student, by example or correction, as to what to see or to say. If he can be given something to say he will then find the means or technique of expressing it. Unless he is original enough to shake off the influence of the teacher, all he can do is to compete with the teacher and his fellow students in preaching the same gospel in new words. The other method gives him the means of saying something and hopes that he will have something original to express.

It is a precocious age in which we live, and too many young people as well as many older ones are being encouraged to build masterpieces first and then learn the trade.

We deal then with only the technical part of watercolor painting, leaving the quarrels between the various schools of painting, with their vague nomenclature and definition of what art is, to take care of themselves, for the moment. Having learned to handle a brush the disciple may then choose his prophet, or be his own prophet, and cry either in one of the choruses or in the wilderness.

In oil painting the thing that one says is of major

importance, but in watercolor painting the manner
of saying it usually counts for more, just as with
prose and poetry. In the one you make a formal
statement—a description, an abstraction, a charac-
terization, even a cartoon,—with carefully chosen
words. In the other the sheer beauty and rhythm
of the words count for more. In our case the brush-
strokes are the words.

A watercolor should not take more than an hour
of intensive work, as far as the actual setting of it
on paper is concerned; but during that hour one
has many things to think of at once. While there is
the matter of color, interpretation, perspective, design, values and intent, involved, each time one
touches a brush to the paper; there is, in addition,
a host of apparently superficial elements like the
question of the amount of water in the brush.

If any of these things can be made as unconscious
or reflex as stepping over a curb or driving a car,
there will be one less encumbrance during the hour
of quick thinking. It is our task to make first one
and then another of these technical procedures reflex, and thus allow ourselves to concentrate on the
more important aspects of painting.

Washington, D. C.   ELIOT O'HARA

MATERIALS REQUIRED

(Total cost, without paper, about $8.00.)

One flat-stroke lettering brush, ox-hair—¾ or 1 inch.

Palette—Eighteen or more depressions for tube colors, or two 10-cent mixing trays.

Medium pencil, piece of art gum.

Two paper spring clips or clothespins to hold paper on a stiff board or corrugated paper, 15 x 22 inches.

Sheets of *rough* watercolor paper, 22 x 30 inch ("Imperial" size), 72 lb. (140 lb. is better but costs more).

The following 18 tubes of watercolors (students' colors—15 or 20 cents a tube—are less expensive, and satisfactory for practice):

COLORS	SUBSTITUTES
1. Orange Vermilion	or Cadmium Scarlet or Vermilion.
2. Alizarin Orange	or Bright Orange No. I or Brilliant Orange No. I.
3. Cadmium Orange	or imitations or equivalents.
4. Cadmium Yellow	or its equivalent in a coal tar (alizarin) color.
5. Indian Yellow	or Gamboge.
6. Lemon Yellow	or Strontian Yellow or Cadmium Pale.
7. Viridian	or a Bright Green, or Hooker's Green.

8. Turquoise ....or Seagreen No. I or Bright Turquoise No. II or Cerulean Blue.
9. Prussian Blue......or Antwerp.
10. Cobalt Blue.......or French or Ultramarine or New Blue.
11. French Blue.......or, if Cobalt is omitted—Mineral or Cobalt Violet.
12. Alizarin Crimson..or Rose Madder or Lake.
13. Burnt Sienna......or Indian or Light Red or Mars Red.
14. Burnt Umber......or Sepia or Vandyke Brown or Mars Orange.
15. Raw Umber.......or Mars Yellow.
16. Lamp Black ....or Ivory, or any Black.
17. Payne's Grey
18. Davy's Grey

NOTE : For a more comprehensive discussion of pigments—their permanence and qualities—see "Making Watercolor Behave," Minton, Balch & Co.

Making
the Brush
Behave

MAKING THE BRUSH BEHAVE

CHAPTER I

ABSTRACT BRUSH DRILL

Six Exercises

WHEN a boxer trains for a fight he doesn't spend all his time in actual boxing, but goes out on the road, running alternately for two minutes and walking for one. Then he jumps rope like a little girl, and after that he may tap a light rubber bag with his forearms and hands. He does other unaccountable exercises which apparently have nothing to do with boxing but which train him for the combat.

In the same way one can train for excellence in brush work by a series of exercises. The lesson which follows is one that should be repeated at intervals, so that the student used to working with charcoal, oils or other media will not follow his natural tendency to hold and use his watercolor brush just as he would another kind of tool.

The Japanese watercolorists of the older school (the ones who do not imitate Paris) have such a course of training. They fill pages with thin conventional lines and other characteristic strokes. These brush exercises are a result of years of practice in doing watercolors according to tradition.

Their great superiority in brush work may be due to their kneeling posture when at work, or their practice of writing with the brush, as well as to their native patience and thoroughness. Although we can adopt the idea of brush training from them, we need a set of exercises adapted to our own use. For this, after examining the best American work in watercolor, I have chosen a set of several movements or frequently used strokes. To these have been added one or two which are purely training for the hand rather than strokes to be incorporated bodily in a picture.

This first lesson is an attempt to make as reflex as possible the use of the brush. After he has practised it enough the student should, without thinking, pick up the right amount of paint as against the amount of water, and he should not need to watch the dryness or the angle of his brush. This, by the way, is the most important lesson to any student used to handling oils, where a prepared paste of fairly even consistency is put on the canvas by only four or five different kinds of short strokes. With watercolor the oil painter must realize and then forget two things: first, that the covering quality of the new medium permits a stroke many times longer than that used in oil; secondly, that the variables in the brush of wetness, strength of color, and speed, permit a flexibility that must be turned to profit. All this holds good, of course, unless one intends to have one's watercolor resemble an oil; in which case one had better use gouache, tempera, or, better still, oil itself.

THE BRUSH DRILL — SIX EXERCISES

The first lesson is divided into six exercises which are a setting-up drill to be repeated occasionally, especially before doing a series of watercolors, or after a lay-off.

The exercises are:

A. Graded Wash.

B. Dry Brushing.

C. Rough and Smooth Strokes.

D. Thin Parallel Lines.

E. Ellipses and S's.

F. Lozenges and Squares.

For these exercises take a half sheet of Imperial rough watercolor paper (about 22″ x 15″), and clip it on a piece of corrugated cardboard of the same size. Beaver board or a drawing board will do. No easel, no preliminary wetting of the paper. With all these exercises use a flat-stroke lettering brush, water and black paint.

A. Graded Wash

By "graded wash" is meant the coloring of an area of paper with a flat, even tone, ranging from white at one side to black at the other.

Draw an uneven pencil line through the middle of the half sheet as a boundary or starting point for the wash.

Wet the brush with pure water, do not give it a shake or press it on the edge of the water jar, as it should be saturated. Holding it vertically, quickly fill in the irregularities of the penciled edge. Tip the paper towards you at an angle of about 20° to horizontal so that a bead of water will form along the edge of the wet place which is nearest to you. On the next stroke add a very slight amount of black paint to the brush charge and move the bead of water towards you by about the width of the brush. (Look out for lumps of paint on the brush; as they will make black streaks.) With long horizontal strokes overlapping the edge of the paper on either side, continue to move the bead of water towards you. As you work add more paint and less water to each brushful. Do not go back into the tinted area more than the width of the brush. It will be necessary to repass several times over the same strip even after it seems evenly coated, because sometimes the depressions in the paper hold air bubbles which are invisible until drying breaks them, when they show in the form of white specks.

By the time you have reached the edge of the paper the wash should have graded into black and the brush will be nearly dry. With the brush wiped dry, take up the drops at the lower edge before they blot back into the partly dry wash.

> *"Drops of water, rain or sweat—*
> *Blot them or balloons you'll get."*
> (CONTRIBUTED.)

When the brush is lightly held you will find that the tips of the brush-hairs, being flexible, will flick down into the depressions and evenly stain them with color. If you press too hard, white specks will

ILLUSTRATION I

Flat versus vertical brush.

The arrows indicate the direction in which the brush moves.

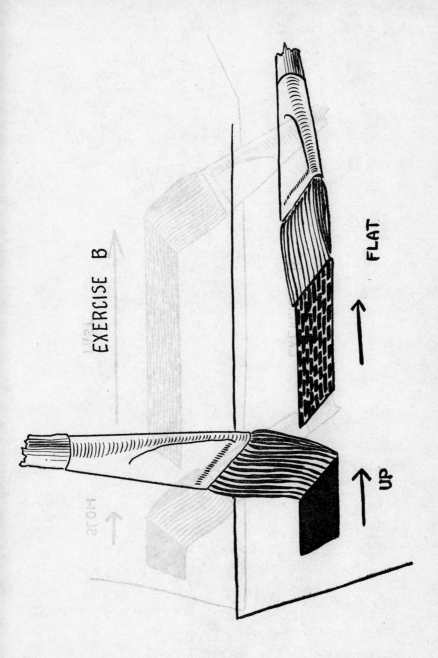

EXERCISE B

FLAT

UP

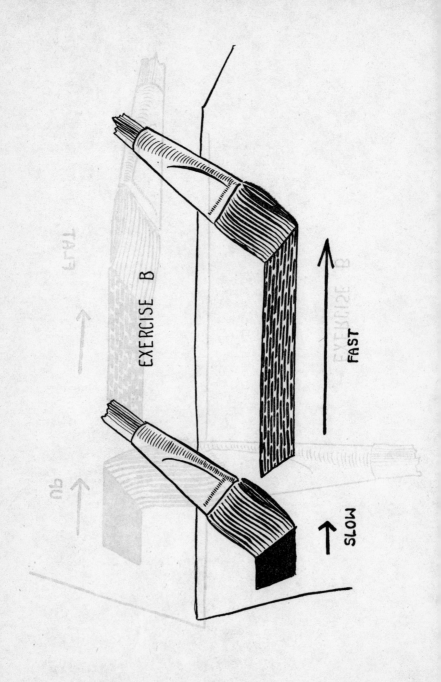

EXERCISE B

FAST

SLOW

ILLUSTRATION II

Fast-moving versus slow-moving brush.

result, as the hairs then bend over and do not present their points to the paper.

An uneven wash will result from uneven wetness of the brush, from too much water on the paper (cured by tipping the paper more), from a particle of solid paint stuck on the brush, or from working so slowly that part of the wash dries before the rest is finished.

B. Dry Brushing

To obtain the effect of "dry brushing" (with a brush which may, when rightly handled, be wet), one takes advantage of the roughness of the paper to color merely the tops of the grains of the surface, leaving the valleys or indentations white. The result is a speckled effect noticeable in many watercolors.

There are three ways of controlling dry brushing:

1. Flat versus vertical brush:—With the brush well-filled with paint move it lightly across the paper, holding the handle vertically. Then move it with the hairs flat on the paper, and you will have a dry brush stroke.

2. Fast-moving versus slow-moving brush:— With the brush medium wet, set it on the paper at an angle of about 45°. Move it slowly, then fast.

Again the second stroke achieves the desired result.

3. Wet versus dryer brush:—You will find that, while the angle at which the brush is held and the speed at which it moves have their effects on the stippling of the paper, the amount of water in the brush is a third variant.

In practising these strokes, try to make them all different and notice that they may be varied by having more or less pigment or color in the brush as well as by the three methods described. You should be able finally to put on at will any kind of stroke, and to do it almost without thinking. Dry brushing is useful for rough surfaces, foliage, sun on water, etc.

C. Rough and Smooth Stroke

This exercise calls for a single stroke which shall be rough or ragged on one side and smooth and even on the other. The contrast, within a single stroke, is achieved by a double use of the brush. For the smooth edge, use the tips of the hairs which, following each other, flip down into the depressions in the paper and stain it evenly. For the ragged edge, press the flat of the hairs which, under the brush, lie along the paper like a board touching the tops of stones.

ILLUSTRATION III

Rough and smooth stroke.

Position for the brush in making a rough and
smooth stroke. The rough side is towards you.

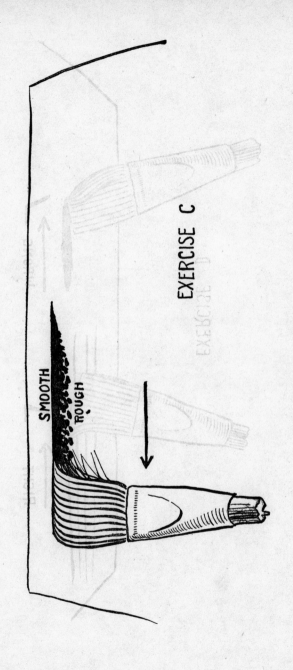

SMOOTH

ROUGH

EXERCISE C

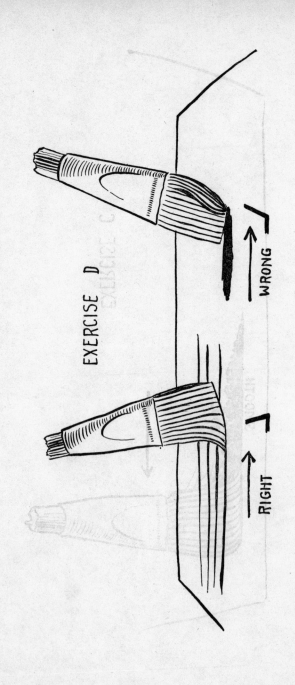

EXERCISE D

WRONG

RIGHT

ILLUSTRATION IV

Angle of brush for thin lines.

Right and wrong way of holding the brush for making thin lines. Notice that the brush should slant the opposite way from a pen.

This rough and smooth stroke works better with right-handed people when run from right to left, especially if the paper is tipped slightly away from one. It is useful for distant tree lines, the shadow side of a rough tree trunk, grass against the sky, and many kindred effects.

D. *Thin Parallel Lines*

The object of this exercise is to train the hand. Holding the brush again like a pencil and starting from the left side of the paper, trail the back corner or left side of the brush; the hairs will stretch out into a thin trail. If the front, or right-hand corner is used, the hairs, instead of trailing out to make a thin line, will bunch up and make a thick one.

Draw perfectly straight, even, thin parallel lines across the entire paper.

E. *Ellipses and S's*

From the fine lines in Exercise D, without changing the angle of the brush, move it towards you, then to the left. The side of an ellipse will be drawn, which, starting from the finest possible line, swells to the full width of the brush and then back to a thin line again.

Repeat, making the various shaped marks shown in the cut. Make them light or dark at will and leave no drops at the ends. You will find most satisfactory a quite dry brush, squeezed out with the thumb and finger of the left hand. There may be much or little paint in the water with which the brush was wet.

F. Lozenges and Squares

These shapes are a further matter of training the brush-hand to get into any kind of corner or angle.

All these exercises should be done with the one-inch brush.

Go back to Brush Drill occasionally, running through the various exercises rapidly on the backs, or even the faces, of spoiled sheets of paper, of which you should shortly accumulate a good number.

Do them in any order; but let each be exactly what you intend it as to value and shape and texture.

Then do them in mixed order, with great rapidity, and alternatingly dark and light.

ILLUSTRATION V

Six exercises in abstract brush drill.

A page of abstract brush drill, showing Exercises A, B, C, D, E and F. Some of these exercises are superimposed as they might be in a painting.

ILLUSTRATION VI

Numbered values.

The numbers are put on all at one time; then the areas are painted in rotation, as each dries. Note that the reflections of the marsh and window were painted too hastily before the large area (6) was dry.

CHAPTER II

VALUES

With Application of Exercises to Landscape

IN our reduction of watercolor to its lowest terms the brush work is to become automatic through practice. Here follows a way of freeing the mind of the second from among these many concerns which entangle us.

Values will always be the most important thing in landscape painting. Most amateur and many professional painters who attempt realistic interpretation of nature (and most of the great painters, conservative and modern, have started as realists) are weak in seeing values.

If the student can, at the outset, train his eye to see and his hand to set down correct values, he will already have an advantage over those who become at once preoccupied with color—design—distortions, and self-expression. These will all assert themselves naturally later on; that is, if he has any real ability.

Select a very simple subject, one that can be

divided into six or seven major areas. Mark the out-
lines of these areas on a piece of paper with a
medium lead pencil. Do not bother with the drawing or detail, as this can be done later with the brush.
Think of your picture at this stage as a map of some
continent with each country outlined, and later to
be filled in with pink, green or blue.

Next ask yourself which of these areas is the lightest in value or the one nearest to white.

In the picture here reproduced (a subject done as
a demonstration for a summer class), all students
agreed that the end of the barn was the lightest area;
therefore a definite black figure 1 was printed on it.
Then came the sky area and other areas. Before you
paint, print the numbers plainly on your paper.
Number 2 will be the next darker, then 3, etc.

If in doubt about two areas, cut two quarter-inch
holes in a dark card and hold the card at the right
distance from one eye so that one spot is on each
area. You then can compare the lightness or darkness of two spots of color. Since they do not relate
pictorially to the areas in question, the mind is not so
apt to deceive the eye with its preconceived notion
of which should be lighter.

Having numbered the areas of your map, start
painting with no. 1, then 2, 3, 4, etc., down to the

darkest. Some sections you will be interested to find will be graded washes (Exercise A); others will be dry brushed or rough and smooth, etc. You will discover that you are again practising brush drill in its application to your outlined areas.

Another reason for numbering the values at the beginning is that a subject is never constant for long at a time. The values, colors, shadows, clouds, etc., shift several times in the hour of work; but the picture must be as of one mood, otherwise it is like a tale told partly in one language, partly in another. A mixed interpretation is in just as bad taste as the trick of throwing gratuitous French phrases into one's conversation.

On finishing the sketch, review it as regards the value of each area. If the lightness or darkness of your areas does not agree with your numbered values you have not succeeded. You will find in water-color that all the colors dry much lighter than they seem when wet. You will have to allow for this tendency, in order to avoid the pale anaemic appearance characteristic of most early work by students.

CHAPTER III

WARM AND COOL COLOR

Its Use in Effects of Sunlight and Distance

IF some colors seem warm and some cool to most of us it is probably because we associate orange and red with fire and blue and green with ice or Maine sea water. In any case most painters assume green-blue to be the coldest; then they pass either way around the spectrum to find first violet and blue, then purple and green, half way; then yellow and red on the warm side with orange for the warmest. (See color diagram, page 67, in Lesson V.)

For this third lesson proceed as with the Values lesson, outlining color areas and numbering values. While the mind may then dismiss values, the warmness and coolness of the colors provide the next stumbling block.

When filling in the areas starting with "1" you will again find that some of them, like clear sky, are graded washes. Other rough surfaces, such as leaves, shingles or gravel, will require one of the dry brush strokes. Each value put on should be darker than its predecessor.

The colors used this time should be Payne's Grey (a cool neutral) and burnt umber (a warm neutral). If an area is blue, pure Payne's Grey should be used; but if it seems to tend either towards green or violet then a little burnt umber should be added to the Payne's Grey. Green and red violet will be half and half, and if there is an orange or red area it should be pure burnt umber.

While the coolness and warmness are entirely independent of the lightness and darkness of the areas, temperature and value both describe them like two different adjectives. It will be difficult to judge the warmness and coldness of certain objects such as rocks or old wood; but judging is your problem. The card with the holes again may help by reducing the areas to two mere spots of gray, of different warmth. Use a black or dark gray card and hold it so that it will not be in the sun.

Think of each sheet of paper as merely an opportunity for experiment, and paint these lessons only because you enjoy doing them. To strive for a good picture with each attempt destroys the carefree and uninhibited frame of mind necessary to the release of your reflexes. You may have noticed that

in a tennis match the relaxed, almost indifferent dev-
otee usually outplays his tense and anxious oppo-
nent. To be well done a thing must seem easily
done. Effort will show in a watercolor more plainly
than in almost any other kind of performance.

Neither should one strive for the quality in painting casually referred to by critics as looseness. Most
good pictures of this kind are good in spite of their
looseness rather than on account of it. This may
sound like heresy in this day of jerry-built masterpieces; but while a tight painter can paint loosely,
on occasion; the reverse is not so often true. Many
famous oil painters work loosely in watercolor simply because they cannot control the medium. To
work in a sloppy way is to imitate the weakness
rather than the obvious merits of these famous painters. For the student, looseness should come, if at
all, naturally and as a by-product, instead of through
carelessness.

Architects often ask to be loosened up in their
watercolor style. The only hope of helping them is
to interest them in other phases of painting. This
process of "de-hibiting"—as we call it at the School
when it succeeds, does so through removing effort
and strengthening reflexes, rather than by painstak-
ing elimination of detail.

CHAPTER IV

TREE STROKES

Differentiation in Texture and Structure

TURN back, before setting out on trees, to the first lesson, Exercise B—Dry Brushing. This will play an important part in doing foliage. You found in that exercise that there were many ways of controlling dry brushing:—the amount of pigment in the water (strength of color); the amount of pigment and water mixed in the brush (wetness); the angle at which the brush is held to the paper; and the speed at which the brush is moved. All of these will be used in tree work, as well as the ragged and smooth strokes and the thin lines.

Find a place where you can see as many different kinds of trees as possible from one point. In most parts of the country a cemetery is ideal, especially an old cemetery. Shade trees have been planted there for years, acorns have taken root, and saplings, planted for ornament, have grown into big trees.

To start your tree practice, divide the paper into

sections, each to contain a tree. Draw, with the pencil first, a straight line for the ground under the tree, and then a single line showing the top silhouette. This is to determine the position of the tree in the picture (in this case, in the section). Then a line for the trunk and one or two lines for major branches. Notice the angle at which the branches attach to the trunk and to one another; the articulations are most important and differ with each kind of tree.

Suppose you have chosen an elm for the first trial: the branches will come out at a V angle. If it is a maple, the angle will be a U, or if it is an oak, a right angle. The branches of the northern spruce slant down, possibly to shed the snow.

These few pencil lines are only an indication of position and structure; most of the drawing will be done with the brush and black paint.

Before beginning to paint look closely at the leaves. If they are small sparse leaves, like those of the willow or birch, a very dry, flatly held brush, will suit the purpose. If they are large, dense leaves, like those of the maple, use a wet brush, moving fairly fast. Notice, also, whether they are dark or light, so that you may get the right strength of color with the water in your brush. Turn your paper up-

ILLUSTRATION VII

Four kinds of trees.

Pine, maple, elm and lilac—differentiated as to branch articulations, branch direction and silhouette.

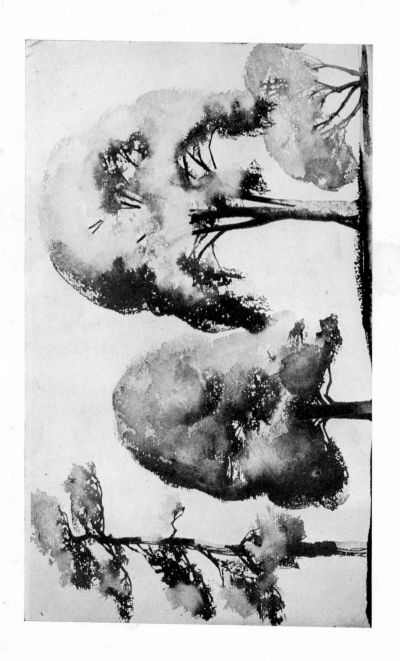

ILLUSTRATION VIII

Trees—differences in structure and foliage.

White pine, Lombardy poplar, arbor vitae and willow. Notice structural differences, leaf sizes, and lightness and darkness of foliage.

ILLUSTRATION IX

Trees—effects through wetness of brush and strength of color.

Trees with five different brush chargings. The color for the bare tree was black, and the brush so dry that the hairs separated into four or five clusters. For the cedar use black, with wetter brush. The other trees were done, respectively, with a wet, light brush, blotted afterwards with a clean, dry brush,—with a light, dry brush,— and with a light, wet brush.

ILLUSTRATION X

Trees—variety through direction of brush movement

Except for the spruce these trees were done with a brush having the same blackness and wetness; but the direction of movement was varied. In all cases the brush was flat on the paper.

side down to fill in the big areas of leaves; in this way it will be easier to get a ragged top edge.

Now turn the paper back and put on the trunk and branches. They will be darker up under the leaves than they are lower down. To impress this on the mind, I have my classes go through the following brief manoeuvre: hold out one hand with the palm down and place the index finger of the other hand against it like the stem of a mushroom or an umbrella. Notice that the tip of the index finger is darker than the rest, where the light from the sky is cut off. A large class of students performing this mystic rite makes a strange sight for the summer visitors in our part of Maine. Do a row of various kinds of trees, exaggerating their differences; then compare them. The cedar will have fine, almost black foliage; while the larch, beech and spruce will all be different in shape, texture and value.

Are there any extra thick branches high up, or are there any branches too heavy for the trunk?

Think of trunk, branches and twigs as conveyors of sap to the leaves, just as a city water system brings water to our homes. A large pipe (the trunk) approaches the city; then, if the city is built all on one street, the big pipe tapers to nothing as uniform smaller pipes serve each house. That is like serving a tall spruce with sap. If there are six suburbs of about equal size a different engineering problem is presented. The willow, for instance, has the large main from the reservoir with a branching out of six or ten large pipes. A tall thin tree or a squat one will have a cunningly worked out skeleton which exactly suits its shape and its requirements for sap.

Trees are something of a problem and should require many hours of practice. Before an attempt is made to paint from memory a maple, for instance, you should have painted many from nature: one with small yellow leaves in the spring; one with heavy green leaves in the summer; one with red leaves in the autumn; and one without leaves in the winter. All of these, in turn, should be on gray days, rainy days, against the light, and with the sun behind you and to one side. Multiply this by the number of kinds of trees and the variety of backgrounds, and you have undertaken a long period of work, even without the next step, which is to modify them to suit your composition without destroying their character.

Paint your trees from nature rather than from other pictures, at first with black, or Payne's Grey and burnt umber. See that they are well differentiated as to value, manner of dry brushing, articula-

ILLUSTRATION XI

The effect of wind on foliage.

The sketch shows the position of the flatly held brush and the arrows the direction of the brush movement. Wind direction is from right to left. Elm, maple and poplar are all done with the brush equally dark and wet.

tion of the branches, proportion and structure. After you have worked on Lesson VII—"Lighting"— come back to trees in color. Make your own application of Lessons VII and VIII to trees, as the same principles of color and lighting are involved in both these later lessons—"Lighting," and "Form by Lighting." But before doing this proceed with Lessons V and VI.

CHAPTER V

THE SPECTRUM

Pigment and Light Primaries

A RAY of light from the noon sun is white (or nearly white) because it contains light of all of the colors together in nearly equal proportions. When the ray is bent by a prism of glass, some parts of the ray are bent more than others. The red part, which has the longest wave-length, is bent the least; then the orange, and so through yellow, green and blue, to the violet part which, having the shortest wave-length, is bent the most. When drops of rain separate these wave-lengths by bending we have the rainbow.

(The names of colors are loosely applied. No two physicists or artists agree, exactly, as to what hue is to be called by a certain name, because the colors pass, by insensible gradations, one into another. The six divisions, however, are usual.)

The various colors or wave-lengths can be separated or strained out of white light by other means.

A substance which we will call vermilion, when white light shines on it, reflects back to our eyes light of the longer wave-lengths, but absorbs strongly light of all the other wave-lengths, so that the red is all that we see. Any substance which produces that effect we call red. Anything which reflects light of the shorter wave-lengths and absorbs the others strongly, we call violet. Grass reflects chiefly light of the medium wave-lengths and is green or yellowish green. Snow reflects all of them and has a white local color.

By mixing together three colored lights—orange, green and violet—in the right proportion, we can obtain the remaining colors; so we may call the three the light primaries (though other triads serve nearly as well). When green and violet light are mixed they give blue; orange and green give yellow; violet and orange give red. In well-equipped theaters these three lights are used; but are called the Ambers, Cyanines and Magentas, instead of orange, green and violet.

Since the hues that we see before we begin to paint come to us by means of light, we must become familiar with the light primaries. When, however, we mix the colors for our picture, we do it with pigments or paint instead of light. The pigment

ILLUSTRATION XII

Diagram showing refraction of a ray of light.

A ray of white light being bent and split into various wave-lengths. The infra-red and ultra-violet, being invisible, need not concern us.

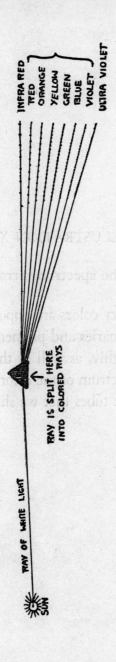

ILLUSTRATION XIII

The colors of the spectrum arranged in a circle.

Complementary colors are opposite each other.
The light primaries and pigment primaries are
indicated roughly, as well as the average position in the spectrum of the colors, by the names
on the tubes that we shall use.

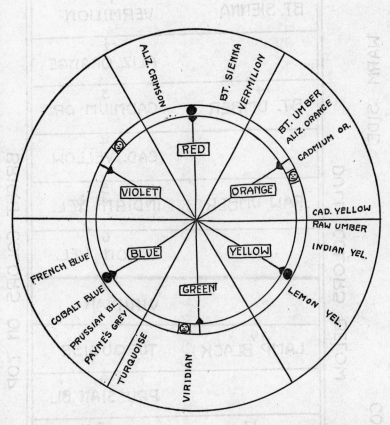

LIGHT PRIMARIES ◉
   MAGENTA
   AMBER
   CYANINE

PIGMENT PRIMARIES ●
   RED
   YELLOW
   BLUE

WARM SIDE

DULL COLORS BELOW

COLD SIDE

13 BT. SIENNA	1 VERMILION
	2 ALIZ. ORANGE
14 BT. UMBER	3 CADMIUM OR.
	4 CAD. YELLOW
15 RAW UMBER	5 INDIAN YEL.
	6 LEMON YEL.
	7 VIRIDIAN
16 LAMP BLACK	8 TURQUOISE
	9 PRUSSIAN BL.
17 PAYNE'S GREY	10 COBALT BLUE
	11 FRENCH BLUE
18 DAVY'S GREY	12 ALIZ. CRIMSON

BRIGHT COLORS ON TOP

ILLUSTRATION XIV

Palette set to separate warm and cold colors.

This arrangement of the pigments on the palette separates the warm and cold colors while retaining the order of the spectrum hues. If the pigments were chosen for their exact place in the spectrum rather than for general utility, you could count six places from any color and find its complement. Such a palette could be made by omitting Prussian blue and Indian yellow and adding a violet and a yellow-green.

primaries are the other three colors—red, yellow and blue. They (as in the case of the former) are called "primaries" because by mixing them all the other colors can be made. Red and yellow paint make orange; yellow and blue make green and blue and red make violet.

The reason for knowing both sets of primaries is shown by a case like the following: a yellow house in shadow has blue sky reflecting into it; thus the two colors, yellow and blue, are involved. Yellow and blue pigments, being primaries, will give green. The unwary painter will wonder why, in his picture, green shadows on a yellow house look wrong; until he realizes that he paints with pigments, but sees in terms of light. Yellow light and blue light do not give green, any more than orange paint and green paint give yellow.

For this lesson take the twelve bright colors in the list and squeeze them out in the order shown (see Illustration XIII). You will notice that the spectrum circle is divided between two reds. This separates the warm colors centering around orange from the cold ones centering around blue. It is a convenient way of disposing them, as we shall find that we are constantly opposing warm and cool color.

It will strike you at once that the brilliant warm

colors are all light in value and the cool ones are all dark. This is an accident of nature and one of the reasons why so many pictures have a bluish appearance. It is because of this weakness of the warm colors in mixtures that I have included in the palette the more neutral but darker warm colors:—burnt sienna (red), burnt umber (orange), and raw umber (yellow). They are less brilliant and are used to darken their more brilliant relatives.

Make sample graded washes of all these colors, showing what their possibilities are; each should go from white, graded almost imperceptibly to the darkest value. A strip of one-inch stripes will suffice, or they may be arranged like twelve pieces of pie, in a circle.

When painting a picture in color adopt the same procedure as in Lesson III, first making pencil indications and numbering values. In coloring, instead of asking yourself "is it warm, cold, or medium?" you will have to ask yourself where in the spectrum circle the color lies. In mixtures between warm and cold bright colors, you will have to favor the warm, because the blues are so dark.

"Remember this and you can't go wrong:
The warm are weak and the cold are strong."

—D. MC CORD.

CHAPTER VI

NEUTRALIZATION

Three Ways of Making Colors Grayer

THE twelve colors making up our rough spectrum were chosen because they were the most saturated or most brilliant ones rather than for their true place in the spectrum. The color chart made in the last lesson shows them in their brightest state, much too bright for most purposes. In painting they will frequently have to be neutralized or made grayer.

There are three ways of doing this:

1. The first way, a very popular method, is to add a little of the complementary color, or the one opposite in the spectrum circle (see diagram on page 67). For instance, if red is wanted slightly grayer add a little green; according to theory as more is added, it gets grayer and finally, passing through gray, becomes a neutral green and at the last a saturated green.

2. The second way of neutralizing a color is to

straddle the bright one. For instance, if an orange yellow is wanted somewhat grayer, the two on either side of it should be mixed. The next two will give an even more neutral orange yellow, until red and green are reached; and as they are, of course, complementary, they give gray.

Both of these methods are uncertain and there are many exceptions, owing to the darkness and lightness of the raw pigments, the fineness to which they are ground, the shape of the particles of paint, or owing to gravity or capillary attraction.

3. But, as in most other cases, there is a simple way of getting gray; and, like most simple methods, it is the surest. In this case it is to use gray paint.

There is a theory now somewhat out of date, but frequently quoted by students and painters, that gray or black should never be used in painting.

Davy's Grey (made of ground slate) is a perfectly inert pigment which mixes well with all twelve of the bright colors. Make the following experiments with Davy's, not Payne's, Grey. With a very dry brush paint a small area of gray on the paper and introduce at one end the slightest trace of any of the twelve bright colors. Blend the two together with a clean and almost dry brush. One end of the patch of color should be light gray; the other of the hue selected; and between them, if they are evenly blended, will be a dozen delicate neutralizations. If too much water is used results will be as muddy as grays produced from complementary colors. Try this with each of the colors, but in the light values only. Black, or the dark warm colors, are better for dark neutrals.

"A little water and lots of color
Keep dull pictures from being duller."
(CONTRIBUTED.)

While mixing patches of color it will be of particular interest to work with the greens. They are usually obtained by mixing the pigment primaries, yellow and blue, and, since all the yellows are light, using plenty of yellow. One should try to get greens which are, at the same time, dark and warm. Any one can get a dark green which is cool; in consequence, such a number do that the world is almost persuaded that it does not see dark warm greens. In the same way, looking at photographs and movies has persuaded this generation that the sky is lighter in value than it really is. We forget that the photographer's plate is color-blind, and lightens the blues but darkens the reds.

Use plenty of yellow orange or raw umber in

making dark greens. Try, moreover, insofar as possible, to mix your colors on the paper rather than on the palette. You will then be relating them to colors already in the picture with which they will have to harmonize.

Pick out a subject with a variety of grays and see in which of the twelve spectral directions each will vary from pure neutral. Here is an exercise in brush work (as always) and in mixing grays. The values, having been numbered again at the outset and painted in order, need not worry you.

> *"To get the best, the purest, blend:*
> *Mix them on the paper, friend."*
> (CONTRIBUTED.)

CHAPTER VII

LIGHTING

Shadows and Reflected Lights

CHOOSE for your subject a light-colored house in an open spot on a sunny day.

The sun's light is white only when it is directly overhead; the nearest approach to this situation is at high noon. In the forenoon and afternoon it is usually yellow, and for perhaps half an hour before sunset it turns orange.

In any case, for most of a sunny painting day we may assume a slightly yellowish light. Everything which is in direct sunlight, then, will have yellow added to its local color. The house in sunlight, having little color of its own, will probably be light. In the case of the illustration, however, the house ranked third in value, as the sky was lighter and the road of clam-shells lightest of all, and labeled no. 1. These sunlit areas will be slightly yellowish or orange: the area that you marked no. 4 might be the roof, the grass, or the road in sunlight, or a part of the sky. For the most part the things with direct sun on them will be lighter than the things in shadow.

Each will have a proportion of its local color and a little yellow from the sun; but it is best to value and color them by eye, when possible, rather than by theory. The theory is to be used only as a help in doubtful cases.

When you come to parts of the house that are in shadow it may be an aid in judging their hue to realize that they are cut off from the sun. No direct rays shine on them. They would be absolutely black, therefore, if it were not that light from the sun, in shining on other things, is reflected back on these shadowed surfaces. In the light which illuminates them there may be blue or green from the sky, white from a cloud, green from nearby grass in sunlight and yellow from the road. The sum of these lights gives you the color which should be added to the local color of the surface in question.

See how many colors you can find in the shadowed parts of a white house. White, having no local color, takes reflected light nicely, and reflects any sunlit thing near or facing it. The sky is always an important factor (there is so much of it); hence the well-worn, but not always true, formula for sun-

ILLUSTRATION XV

Adaptation of hues and values to lighting.

This illustration, like the others in this book, is a photograph of an actual demonstration painted for thirty or forty students, and does not pretend to be a finished picture. Note the graded washes, dry brushing, rough and smooth strokes, and fine lines.

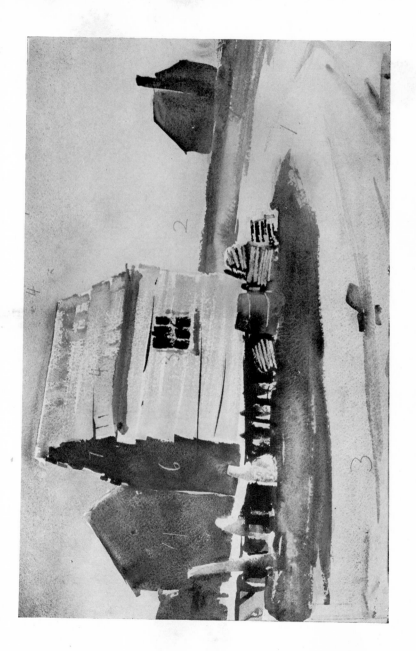

"Gulls, Monhegan," by Eliot O'Hara

light: "Orange for the light, and its complement, blue, for the shadows."

The law for illumination of a surface is that its brightness varies inversely as the square of the distance away. This means that while the sky is constant in its influence on a shadow, other surfaces in sunlight throw their color into the shadow only if they are fairly close. A yellow road in sunlight will affect the lower part of the shadowed side of the house more than the upper part. The side of the house will be a graded wash, bluer at the top, if the sky is blue, but lighter and with some orange, lower down, where the road reflects into it. Under the eaves there will be no light from the sky,—only light from the road.

While working, remember to keep the paper in shadow, to approximate indoor conditions. With the paper in the glare of the sun, incidentally, it is very easy to get a kind of painter's snow blindness and headache, as the eyes were not meant for such a strain.

> *"Here's a good one:*
> *Your back to the sun."*

—D. MC CORD.

Exaggerate all differences in value and hue, because, when the picture is taken into the house, it

will be illuminated by only one or two windows or
an electric light, instead of by the reflected light
from the entire sky.

Failure to allow for this difference between out-
door and indoor light makes many pictures look
dead and gray.

In the matter of lighting, as well as in all other
phases of painting, never deviate from the point of
view that your picture is the important thing,—
more important than any laws of nature or rules that
any one has conceived. Technique is a mere tool, as
are composition and color harmony. But they are
tools to be used with knowledge, not by guess work.

You, for the moment, are the creator and need
give no reasons or explanations for what you do in
building your pictures.

You go to nature for suggestions, not for something to reproduce or copy. These lessons, and all
teaching of art that is of value, can provide only an
understanding of the elements that suggest to you
patterns, colors and emotions.

CHAPTER VIII

FORM BY LIGHTING

Rocks in Terms of Geometric Shapes

PILE up four or five stones of various shapes in a way that will let the sun shine on one side of each; choosing light-colored gray or white, and yellow or reddish, rocks.

In mapping out your picture with a pencil make the rocks into definite geometric shapes:—a ball, a cylinder, a pyramid, a cone or a cube.

Before numbering the values, draw a black arrow showing the direction of the sun. You should arrange this "still life" so that the sun will come from one side.

There will be five elements of lighting present on each rock, as follows:

A. The rock in sunlight.
B. The shadow part facing the sky.
C. The shadow part facing another rock.
D. The black crack under the rock.
E. The cast shadow of it on the next rock.

ILLUSTRATION XVII

Form through lighting.

The two arrows at the top of this demonstration show the direction of the sun. The graded wash above is blue. On the ball the surface looks rough on account of the dry brushing between A and B.

"RANCHOS CHURCH," Oil Painting by Georgia O'Keefe

Whereupon the sequence is repeated, in exactly the same order, with the next rock.

If the rock has a rough surface the edge between A and B will be dry brushed (see Exercise 3, Lesson I). This is because each little lump on the surface has a light and a shadow. The edge between the sky shadow B and the reflected light C will be a graded wash.

The edge between the cast shadow E and the sunlight on the next rock A will be a hard even line.

The picture, when finished, will be a highly conventionalized series of forms arranged to make a composition. One school of painters has become so interested in subjects of this kind that they have built up around them a cult, the cult of form, to the exclusion, at times, of other considerations. Some of Georgia O'Keefe's simplifications, as well as Charles Sheeler's pictures were probably done because the painter was, for the moment, interested in seeing form through lighting.

If the sun is behind you, A and D will be more visible than B, C and E; that is, you will see chiefly sun-lighted rocks and dark cracks.

If the sun is in front of you the A or sunlit part will be reduced to mere edges and you will see much of the shadow and reflected light and many cracks.

After completing this study paint a realistic, loosely done, rock picture by throwing in at random a color which will be an average or least common denominator of all the A's or lighted areas; then, over that, splashes of B's and C's or shadows. The next darker will be the E's or cast shadows. At this point, however, you should place them carefully, instead of throwing them in. Look for a place on your paper which might be a rock and make it into one by giving it a cast shadow with a black crack underneath.

Utilize, but do not abuse, any knowledge of lighting acquired by doing the formalized still life pictures of rocks. There will be a temptation to put in too many cracks and spots of color.

Do not attempt actually to draw any special rock unless it dominates the picture or can be given a shape interesting enough to merit this attention.

> *"To make the critics smile and dimple*
> *Keep your composition simple."*
>
> (CONTRIBUTED.)

N O T E : After having done this lesson go back and do trees in color, making use of your experience gained in the lighting of houses and rocks. (See Lesson IV.)

CHAPTER IX

TREE SHADOWS ON A WHITE HOUSE

Use of Shadows to Show Form

TAKE a piece of paper or cardboard and cut in it small quarter-inch holes of all shapes: squares, slots, triangles, crescents, stars, etc. Then prop up your watercolor paper facing the sun. If you hold the perforated card a foot away from it, all the queer-shaped holes will cast light spots of exactly the shape and size of the holes. Now move the perforated card ten feet or more away from your watercolor paper but still let it cast its shadow on the paper. (To accomplish this you may have to stand on a chair or hill-slope.) You will find that each hole or chink, whatever its shape be, will now cast a perfectly round, light spot.

Trees, with light sifting through them, do exactly this when they cast their shadows on house or grass.

Now turn the watercolor paper at several different angles to the perforated card. The circles will lengthen into ellipses and the axes of the ellipses

ILLUSTRATION XIX

Tree shadows on a white house.

The black lines on the grass, bath-house, trees and more distant house and roof, are indications of the axes of elliptical sun-spots. It will be found easier to hold the brush always pointing away from you and rotate the paper until the directional line is at right angles to the brush, before doing any given set of ellipses.

will take various directions according to the angle of the paper.

This preliminary experiment is to impress on the mind what happens when the sun shines through irregular interstices in the trees; with the end that you will look for circles and ellipses when painting.

Choose a white house for your subject, preferably with the trees casting their shadows on the grass or road, on two sides of the house and on the roof.

Number the values as if it were all in sunlight and paint it that way.

Then, before superimposing the shadows, draw a line on each side of the house, on the roof and on the grass, showing the direction taken by the axes of the ellipses. (A circle in perspective is an ellipse.)

When painting the shadow, look first for the reflecting surface which is lighting it—sky? grass? road? Choose the colors and move the brush in an elliptical way along the directions noted. The shadow should be an evenly graded surface with lighter spots in it. The shape of these spots, their direction and the way they "snowplow" or "V" at the corner of the house or roof, should be part of your means of showing the form of the house.

Ellipses do not make a well-represented house

with shadows, and a well-represented house does not make a work of art; but, for the moment, it is mere technique in which we are interested. We are only sharpening our tools in these fourteen lessons.

Where a tree with heavy foliage cuts off the sky's light from a shadow, it will have less blue in it and be blacker.

When the road and grass in front of the shaded house are themselves in shadow they cannot throw a reflected light into the shaded house.

What would a brick walk in sunlight do to the shaded house?

Would a mass of leaves a few feet from the house cast light ellipses on it?

It is easy to let this kind of subject get very complicated. Try to preserve as many large simple areas as possible and do not let the paper be covered with elliptical scroll-work.

A simple composition is always more difficult to achieve than a complicated one because it is unclothed. Adornment and padded shoulders cannot improve a good figure. The next time you go to a general watercolor exhibition find a picture where the whole page is covered with either clever and facile brush-strokes or intentional runs and blobs. Mentally undress it and see what you have left.

"Behind much busy brush-work lurks
A man who composition shirks;
But clever brush-work often saves
Bad watercolors from good graves."

(CONTRIBUTED.)

N O T E : Repeat Lesson VIII with houses instead of rocks.

CHAPTER X

RECESSION INTO SPACE

Illusions of Distance

WHEN rain is falling, or the air is full of fog, the effect is as if a series of equally spaced gauze curtains were interposed between the eye and things included in the sketch. The more distant things like mountains, distant tree lines, etc., are naturally more obscured than the nearby things. Even on a clear day there is a difference in value and color, dependent on distance. This is probably due to water-vapor or dust in the air.

To impress on the mind the various methods for making a thing look distant, draw a line across the middle of the paper and plan two sketches—duplicates, as far as the drawing is concerned.

Number the values of one of the sketches and paint it exactly as you would if it were a single picture (as in Lesson VII). Having completed it, turn to the other and paint the sky and most distant land or trees exactly as they are in the first sketch—the same value and color. The immediate foreground also should be a duplication of the first.

You have now fixed limits in space or nearness to you between which all the other items will be placed, just as a frame fixes vertical and lateral limits.

All pictures have the "fore and aft" limitation of recession, either arranged consciously by the painter, just as he chooses the limits of the frame,—or in spite of him.

The problem of this lesson is to make all intermediate things in this picture between these limits move back, away from you, by means of aerial or painter's perspective, and without recourse to ordinary perspective, which is concerned with vanishing points and with making things smaller as they recede.

There are four ways by which this painter's perspective or recession is usually achieved. More distant things are:

1. Paler.
2. Bluer.
3. Less detailed.
4. Less differentiated as to light and shadow.

There are a few exceptions, such as the warmer distance when looking through a mist or smoke

ILLUSTRATION XX

Double sketch—to demonstrate recession.

In the top picture an attempt was made to have the distant land, sky and foreground at the same distance as they are in the lower picture. Everything else has been pushed back.

LIMITS OF RECESSION

LIMITS OF RECESSION

"La Maison dans les Pins," by Cézanne

towards the setting sun; but they are so few that many painters, almost without forethought, use the cool colors to denote distance and the warmer ones for proximity.

I suggested, in Lesson VII, exaggerating all differences in value and hue. Distance, too, may be exaggerated. In fact many painters make the edge of a cylindrical tree-trunk or arm a trifle bluer merely because it is not as near to the eye as the center.

By observing these formulæ (and formulæ are a part of technique but not of art) you can definitely place in space any item in the picture. Indeed, this placing of things in space and making planes recede or approach or interweave may become an obsession with you as it has with countless recent painters. It has interested Cézanne, intrigued many, made a few famous, and ruined a host.

NOTE: Cézanne, in his pictures, has often utilized recessions within small areas. For example, with trees or squares of cultivated land, the plowed field, two miles distant, may be painted with the same strength of color and recession within itself that is used for an area in the foreground or intervening distance. Thus, although alike, each recedes individually. One is tucked behind another by fading, as in Japanese watercolors of mountains, or they are staggered in a way that gives the illusion of their going back. In my own "Rio Frias in the Andes," the peaks, while of the same hue and value, appear to recede.

This use of receding planes is another branching off point from realistic painting from nature, such as the arrangements of forms described in Lesson VIII. It may appeal to you as a means of expression you may wish to adopt.

It is to be regretted that the illustration on page 99 which, like similar ones in this book, is a mere demonstration, cannot be reproduced in color, or even in its true values, to illustrate the exercise more clearly; but colored plates would have placed this set of lessons out of the reach of many students.

"God save the Queen! Long live the King!
Perspective is a pleasant thing:
It keeps the windows back of sills,
And puts the sky behind the hills."
—D. MC CORD.

CHAPTER XI

REFLECTIONS IN WATER

Angle of Vision, Refraction

LET us approach this problem of reflections in water first by assuming that everything which is to be painted has a more or less rough or lumpy surface, whether it be a stone wall having stone-sized lumps, or a painted house having brush-marks in the paint or grain in the wood. Further, let us assume that outdoors the light falls from above, so that the tops of the lumps are lighter and the underneath parts darker, or in shadow. Both are fairly safe assumptions.

When we look straight across the water at the lumps or roughness on a house or boat we see a certain proportion of light as against dark. If we were to swim down in the water and look up at them, we would see less of the light and more of the dark. Since it is from the water that our reflection comes, one might be led to suppose that things in the air are usually lighter than the same things seen reflected in water. The supposition is partly true.

There are, however, other influences at work. The water may have color like the red of mill ponds or the Volga, the green of Bermuda or the Mediterranean, or the yellow of the Ohio. Notice that the darker reflections partake more of the color of the water than the lighter ones. In smooth water a light sky will be hardly any darker in reflection than in actuality.

Water often has oil or scum or floating particles on it which reflect light. Watch carefully for the way in which this scum affects the relationship between various reflected elements. It may draw them all towards neutral or it may color them all slightly with green or some other hue. It may darken the values of the lights and at the same time lighten the values of the darks, as if they were seen through a screen.

The color of the bottom will show up, though not evenly, through shallow water. It will be more noticeable nearby, where you look down into the water, than at a distance, where the angle of incidence is small. It will, moreover, be more apparent in the dark reflections than in the light ones.

When the water is flat, like a mirror, we see perfectly repeated what is above. The trees, houses, hills, etc., however, do *not* repeat themselves *from the edge of the water,* as that edge is only an arbitrary one governed by the shore line. They repeat their length *from the point at which they would meet the water,* if the water were continued on to a point directly under them.

If the water is ruffled we look into the top or near side of the ripple or wave, and what we see is correspondingly low or high. The top will reflect the low sky or the trunk of a tree; the near side will reflect the high sky or the tip of the tree. The far side of the wave is hidden from us and so reflects nothing.

Remember that ripples or waves have perspective like ties of a railroad track. Now mutilate your picture by drawing a pair of tracks leading to the horizon, and mark in the ties. Do they correspond in size to the waves? The hope is that the mutilated picture will recur to you the next time you see waves.

Waves all have a direction, usually a series of ellipses starting from a focal point. The ellipses being in perspective are flatter on their far side. They might be drawn in as directional lines, merely for the brush-strokes, like the ones showing the direction of the sun-spots in Lesson IX.

The question of reflections is fairly intangible and varies almost with each picture. You may find that you prefer to put in the brush-strokes while the preliminary wash is still wet, or you may prefer to wait until it dries. In any case, it is better to complete the top part of the picture first, putting in the reflections after there is something to reflect. With the reflections, as with the object reflected, be sure to apply the lighter tones first, reserving the darker until afterwards.

CHAPTER XII

MEMORY SKETCHING

By Use of "Quickies"

CUT the paper in two with a pencil line as in Lesson X. Then cut one of the halves in two. This will make one large and two small rectangles.

Choose a subject and with the pencil draw in the major areas, using one of the smaller rectangles. Number the values. Time yourself while doing this and do not spend more than five minutes on it.

Then in the second rectangle paint very roughly and without pencil lines areas of color corresponding to the ones marked out in the first values sketch. The areas of color may be of the right value and may somewhat resemble in shape the features of the landscape before you. These color spots are mere reminders of what you are looking at. If need be, leave white spaces around them to prevent their running together, or let them run. Think of yourself as spreading out a set of samples very quickly. Let that be the sky and that, the roof, and this dry-brushed loop, the tree, with this dark running into it on the shadow side.

This second sketch with color patches is known among my students as a "quickie"; and this, too, should be limited to five minutes.

Now for the third period of five minutes, simply look at the subject. Memorize the details, reflected lights and textures. Make notes on the two small rectangles, writing in "darker," "bluer," "more neutral," "distant," or any words that will be reminders of possible changes. The "looking," however, is the most important.

Having spent fifteen minutes before the subject (and, if you should spend more, the value of the lesson is spoiled), move to a distant place hidden from the subject or anything similar to it, or go home and work indoors.

No peeking! You should now, in the third or largest rectangle, produce a watercolor, referring only to the values sketch, the "quickie" and your mental notes.

You have presumably chosen a shady, comfortable spot to work in; you have an hour ahead of you, and expectation for a good piece of work should run high.

Your memory is intended to act as a sieve, sifting

out the details which contribute to the characteriza-
tion, and forgetting those which do not.

You will not be obsessed with copying nature, and
may take liberties with the arrangement and colors
already set down. Your object should be to record
sincerely your own reaction to the subject.

I sometimes find that on this lesson the class will
be inverted: the students who have made good pictures, when easy reference to the subject was possible, producing failures; and many who, until that
time, had not done well, turning out excellent pictures. Such students should be induced to work more
from memory.

Memory sketching on some such plan as this is
a regular procedure with many American and Eng-
lish watercolorists. They often come home from a
trip with no pictures at all, but instead, sheaves of
hotel note paper or numbers of pocket note-books,
covered with shorthand reminders decorated with
extraordinary symbols and hieroglyphics which they
alone can interpret.

The Japanese of the old school do most of their
work from memory, without the aid of values
sketch, "quickie" or written notes; but after hours
of looking.

In memory sketching as done in this lesson many

ILLUSTRATION XXII

A group of "quickies," or color notes.

The values drawing in the middle was done at the same place as the "quickie" to its right and the one in the lower left corner.

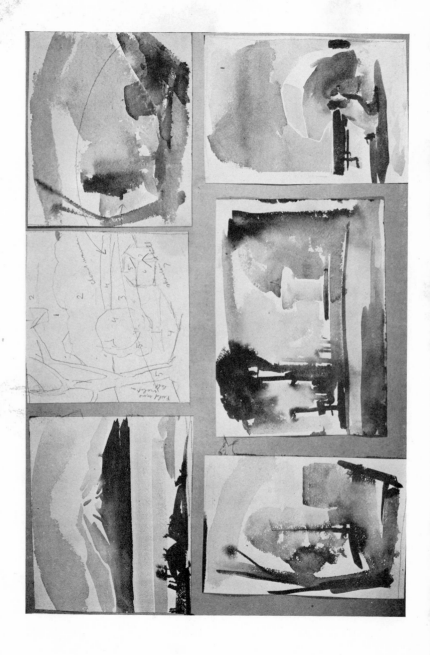

"Franconia," by John Marin

students will find that their "quickie" is finer in color and composition than the resulting picture. It may be worth while for them to do a series of the five-minute sketches. Ideas for larger pictures will develop from them. Or, if the painter can stand the cost of reams of watercolor paper, he may take a large brush and do a series of enlarged "quickies"; some of which may be good enough to exhibit.

This rapid setting down of impressions marks a third point of departure from representational painting, like the two mentioned respectively in Lessons VIII and X.

The speed of working in this manner is an advantage as it records a mood which is transient, whether it be a mood of nature or of the painter or a combination of the two,—a recording by someone of his feeling towards his subject.

Students who enjoy doing "quickies" should look at the work of John Marin and his imitators. He must work very fast, from the amount of apparently involuntary dry brushing in his pictures. I have never seen him paint, but my guess is that he does an enormous quantity of watercolors in about fifteen or twenty minutes each, and saves only the ones he likes.

As the element of chance plays a large part in any

such rapid production, the number of successes will be proportionally few, although perhaps more spontaneous, in relation to the number among the controlled watercolors that we are actually studying.

CHAPTER XIII

CHANGES IN COLOR AND LIGHT

Forecasting Transitions at Sunset

BEFORE proceeding with this lesson please reread Lesson V on the Spectrum.

Pictures in a late light or at sunset are among those almost as often "muffed" as attempted. Let us start then as in the earlier lesson with an analysis of light, but this time of the light which illuminates the landscape late in the day. The wave-lengths of light from the sun are bent, as has already been shown, by a glass prism or by drops of water, dust, etc., which are a part of the earth's atmosphere. The shorter wave-lengths are bent more than the longer ones. Thus it happens that in coming through the earth's atmosphere some of the shorter wave-lengths are lost or scattered. This "selective scattering" (as the physicists call it) is naturally more noticeable late in the day than at noon, because the sun's light has to pass through more atmosphere when it approaches diagonally. The violet light (the shortest wave-lengths) is, of course, the first to be scattered and dissipated, then the blue. Without these cold colors the sun's light looks warmer. There now remains most of the green, yellow, orange and red light. It illuminates clouds and other things with a yellowish light because green and orange are light primaries and make yellow when mixed; to this is added the original yellow light and the red. As the sun sinks lower and traverses still more atmosphere the next shorter green wave-lengths are scattered, leaving yellow, orange and red. The result is an orange light. Then the yellow goes, and finally the orange followed by the red.

Notice that the definite cycle of colors, lighting a cloud at sunset, follows the order of the spectrum. Starting with white it turns yellow, then orange, then red, and lastly dark. At this point it is usually seen against a green sky and in consequence looks purple.

The white has, naturally, the longest duration (all day), the yellow the next longest, and the red the shortest. If you see a cloud as yellow, for instance, paint it orange. If you see it orange, paint it red; because, by the time you get it on the paper and are ready to put on the sky color which goes with it, it will be red. You thus forecast nature's changes and, if you can work fast enough, get a true relationship.

Since there are nearly always clouds of different altitudes, the high ones are frequently white or yellow, while the lower ones are orange or red; but a high cloud will go through the same sequence.

It is unfortunate that our lives are planned on a schedule that often brings us to the dining room just at sunset. If you can defy tradition and attend a few sunsets, you should convince yourself of this extraordinary cycle by checking the colors of several clouds as they pass through it. Any sunset will serve.

While the clouds are running half through the spectrum, another predictable phenomenon is taking place simultaneously: the clear sky is going through a change in color which is spatial as well as temporal.

If we were in the stratosphere where there is no dust or water-vapor, the sky would be black. During the day the sun's rays strike it at an angle which deflects earthward the short blue wave-lengths. As the sun gets lower, the horizon or lower sky begins to be turquoise, then green, the blue being crowded into the zenith. Yellow then replaces the green and that in turn becomes orange, then red, purple, violet and blue. The last two colors show very late and usually only at or near the horizon. At times, how-

ever, all the colors may be crowded by a wide ex-
panse of one of the middle ones into the very top
of the picture, or, on the other hand, they may grow
out of the area near the horizon.

Notice the sequence of the colors in this giant
back-drop, gradually rising: blue, green, yellow,
orange, red, violet and blue. (A perfect spectrum,
although quite pale and dependent on mist and cli-
matic conditions for its emphasis on any particular
hue.)

After reading this chapter it might be well to
observe a few sunsets and to try to analyze them,
before beginning to paint one.

When you are about to begin, have ready freshly
squeezed-out paint and a big brush and be prepared
to work faster than you have with any other subjects.

A sunset is only an enlarged "quickie." The
clouds, while lighted as described, sometimes have
a shadow side and reflected lights, and cast shadows
on one another.

Other items in the landscape in silhouette against
the sky will, of course, be dark and lighted only by
reflections from sky or clouds facing them. These
dark items will probably have to be noted as to
value and hue and put in later, because dusk is a
slow drying-time for watercolor. The sky and

clouds, painted in not over ten minutes, will take perhaps twenty minutes to dry.

The clouds may be dry-brushed as to edges or blended; they are nearer than the sky and may have detail. The clear sky itself, as always, is the most distant thing in the picture and as such will have to show no detail or irregularities, but be a pure, evenly-graded wash. A rough-hewn sky—in a water-color—comes close to us and fuses with other areas. Such a fusion or overlapping of distant ones with nearer ones may be done in the interests of composi-tion, but should be by intention, not by accident or the stupid application of standard-sized brush-strokes to all parts of the picture.

It is usually fatal to put the sun itself into a pic-ture, since—the source of all light—it must be so much higher in value than anything else,—the dark red balls of the nineties to the contrary notwith-standing.

CHAPTER XIV

REVIEW

With a Few Notes on Organization

IN the thirteen lessons preceding I have avoided any teaching of Art and have scrupulously adhered only to subjects having to do with technique. Subjects for the experimental pictures have been dictated by the need of working out some problem of lighting or some technical difficulty. The skill acquired will be applicable to almost any style of work.

In the borderland between technique and painting as it is taught, there are a few of the more obvious and traditional precepts. The first might be a word in general as to the study of watercolor. If these lessons of mine have helped with the superficial or mechanical part of watercolor painting that is all they were intended to do. So far rules, formulæ and standard procedures are proper, just as a study of physics and chemistry gives the groundwork to an inventor. While he has no rules for the creative part of his task, he may get ideas or starting points from other people.

It will help you to study art with a variety of different kinds of teachers. Get something from one and more from another; move quickly to the next school and keep a firm hand on your own reins, if you do not wish to be an imitator. If you were to spend a period of years studying with one painter you would grow to be like him, and might even surpass him in his own line. Before choosing a master and committing yourself to a period of influence under him,—ask yourself if you liked four years ago the same things that you like now, and what you might like four years hence.

I have mentioned, in the various lessons, that the preliminary pencil lines served merely to locate areas on the paper. Plan with a pencil, but paint with a brush. Before mapping out a picture and numbering the values it may be profitable to make several very small sketches of various aspects and points of view. This will help you to decide, for instance, whether the subject lends itself to a horizontal or vertical rectangle, and what kind of rectangle. A few such "thumbnail" sketches are shown here illustrating the quality of balance.

BALANCE

1. In the first the house on the left is too heavy to balance the bush. The boys on the see-saw are a way of illustrating this.

2. Again two heavy objects have nothing to balance them (a favorite mistake with beginners).

3. This picture has better balance.

4. Two heavy objects on either side of the picture balance obviously, but fall down in being too obvious.

5. A heavy object nearby may often be made to balance a lighter one in the distance. Diagonal balance of areas, spots of the same color or value, or items of equal interest, is preferable to lateral or vertical balance.

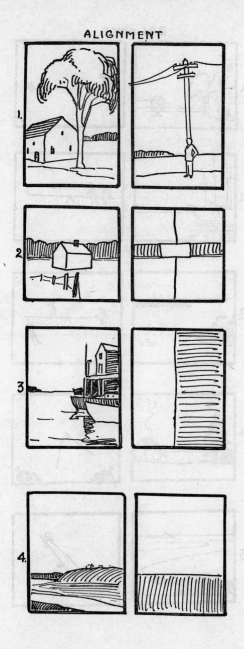

1. It is unfortunate that the trunk of the elm tree coincides with the edge of the house. The elm should not shoot up from the eaves any more than the telegraph pole should grow out of the man's head. Nature need not force art to accept all of her juxtapositions.

2. When a distant tree line is allowed to prolong the ridgepole of the house one seems like a continuation of the other. The placing of both the house and horizon, moreover, half-way across the paper, is a poor choice of position in anything except a very formal design, such as a stained glass window.

3 and 4. Filling half the paper and leaving the other half empty is as bad as planting an object in the middle. Dividing the paper into thirds or fifths provides a set of strong positions. The theory of dynamic symmetry also has several ways of determining positions, directions and areas within rectangles. Better than any formula, however, is an instinct for what is right.

1. The wedge of the beach and the cloud become arrowheads pointing to the left, as shown by the black areas on the sketch at the right. These are "unrequited" arrows and give a sense of motion that should be counteracted in some such way as that shown in the two sketches below.

2. The palm trunks and bank form a series of diagonals all tipping to the right. The attempt to hold them up in the two following sketches is not successful because, while opposite diagonals are supplied, the white areas may unfortunately be thought of as representing a path of descent for these falling diagonals. Can you draw these three slanting lines within the rectangle and then supply other lines or areas that will give them real support?

3. Just as an arrowhead in (1) pushes on out of the picture, a parenthesis or curved line or edge holds back. In the picture of tree and bush and in the sketch to the right an assumed force is being held back. The lower plan on the left is better; the one on the right with the parenthesis and arrowhead, not quite as good.

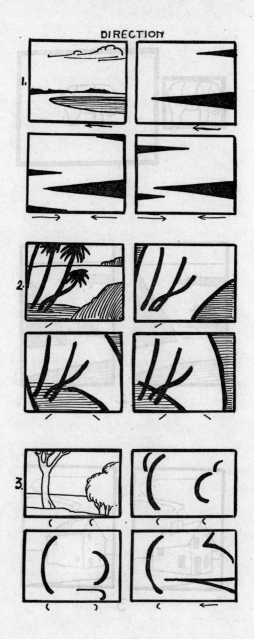

SCALE

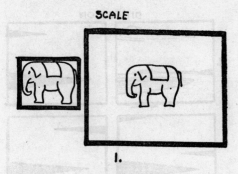

1.

2.

3.

1. The two elephants were drawn equal in size, but a thing seems larger when it nearly fills the paper or surrounding area. There are various ways of using illusions of this kind to give scale or implied size to an element in a picture.

2. One may, for instance, paint in an object of known dimensions. The cliff is the same size in each picture, but the inclusion of the duck or the ocean liner can make it vary from two feet to a quarter of a mile. In a picture of a hand holding a 50-cent piece the hand could be made to look larger by keeping the size of the coin the same but making it five cents and painting a buffalo on it. And, to be utterly absurd, suppose the buffalo realistically enough painted to look alive. That would make the hand twenty feet across.

3. A more serious use of scale is in determining the size of windows in a house. The two houses are the same, but the one on the left looks like a small house on account of its wide eaves, large chimney and windows. In this case one assumes the size of a person who could go in at the door to be of normal height. How would you make a person going up steps seem to be of small stature?

Deceiving the eye of the observer is part of the technique of giving scale to your picture.

RHYTHM

1. A simple line or area cannot have rhythm.

2. When two of them are shown they still do not have it because rhythm is a spacing of units or repetition of emphases.

3. With three or more units there can be rhythm. If all the units are alike in size and shape, however, their monotony tires the mind.

4. To please, the lines should be near enough alike in size, shape and position so that the mind will at once find amusement in sorting and relating them. If, by any trick of spacing, suggestion, or purposely incomplete arrangement, you can challenge the mind of the observer, then he begins to share in your creation and is won.

This effort, by every means of technique or trick of veiled suggestion, to induce the observer to share with you in realizing the emotional content of your picture, is of the utmost importance, up to the point where you give him too much to do. When he begins to realize that instead of building with you, he is being asked to work out a puzzle, then he turns against you, especially if you yourself do not

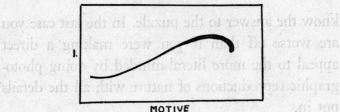

MOTIVE

DUPLICATION

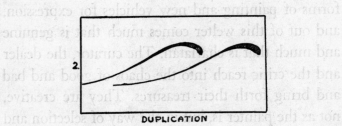

REPETITION

RHYTHM

know the answer to the puzzle. In the last case you are worse off than if you were making a direct appeal to the more literal-minded by doing photographic reproductions of nature with all the details put in.

Painters, the creative ones, go on inventing new forms of painting and new vehicles for expression, and out of this welter comes much that is genuine and much that is charlatan. The curator, the dealer and the critic reach into the chaos of good and bad and bring forth their treasures. They are creative, not as the painter is, but in the way of selection and of judgment; to this they add a quality of salesmanship which consists of their ability to win public approval and acceptance. Like investment brokers who sell bonds, there are conservative ones who have traditional offerings and work on that section of the public which has fear of the new and unusual. There are also the speculative ones who play on the public's fear of being thought old-fashioned or behind the times.

Both kinds of dealers, curators and critics, sell good pictures and promote good painters. Of the bad which both sorts of dealers also sometimes sell, the first will err on the side of old chromos, the second, on the side of fakes.

The dealers are the campaign managers of the painters. With public men, their ability to govern should be the measure of their success rather than their ability to get themselves elected. And so with painters, their "salability" or lack of it, should not affect the evaluation of their work. It may be too much to hope that each person will judge painting independently and without help any more than that he will vote without the aid of current events speakers or newspapers. We have an unfortunate wish to be on the winning side; but you, at least, starting out on a career of painting, can steel yourself to listen to your own likes and dislikes, and can be honest in expressing your opinions on the works of others, and in either preserving or destroying your own good or bad sketches.

It will obviously help you to see as many watercolor exhibitions as there are in your neighborhood and to read all the current criticism in the art publications and papers; but do not believe all that you read in either the papers or the books, such as this volume. You have your own criteria and standards, or will build them for pictures, just as you have for morals or politics, and your independence is the thing that you must safeguard.

Just as there are fashions in art that come and go,

there is also a definite lag between the discerning section of the art commentators and producers and others less independent. Much of today's criticism and comment is just as dated as the bustle.

The work of winning the country over to less traditional forms of art which began twenty years or so ago was timely, and at that period independent and original; but now that the painters, critics, curators, art students, teachers and bourgeoisie have been freed from what was then traditional, the latest converts find themselves again sounding as obvious as the die-hards of the last era.

Tradition has laid a new length of track into what was unexplored mining land, and the railhead is swarming with tenderfeet persuading one another that they discovered it. The real pioneers are probably engaged further out,—or are reviewing the field to see if a good vein has been overlooked, or are assaying the treasure in the hope that they may find out how much fool's gold was at first supposed as real as the vast wealth of undeniably genuine.

A PARTIAL BIBLIOGRAPHY
OF USEFUL BOOKS FOR
THE WATERCOLORIST

A Theory of Pure Design, Denman W. Ross, Ph.D. Houghton, Mifflin & Co., 1897.

On the Laws of Japanese Painting, Henry P. Bowie. Paul Elder & Co., 1911.

Painting and the Personal Equation, Charles H. Woodbury, N.A. Houghton, Mifflin & Co., 1919.

The Technique of Water-Colour Painting, L. Richmond, R.O.I., R.B.A., and J. Littlejohns, R.B.A., R.B.C., A.R.W.A. Isaac Pitman & Sons, 1925.

The Art of Water-color Painting, E. Barnard Lintott. Charles Scribner's Sons, 1926.

British Water-colour Painting and Painters of Today, J. Littlejohns. Isaac Pitman & Sons, 1931.

Practical Water-color Sketching, E. G. Lutz. Charles Scribner's Sons, 1931.

Making Watercolor Behave, Eliot O'Hara. Minton, Balch & Company, 1932.

Making a Water-colour, George Pearse Ennis. The Studio Ltd., 1933.

Studies in Water-colour, Leonard Richmond. Sir Isaac Pitman & Sons, Ltd., 1933.

A Manual on Water-colour Drawing, L. A. Doust. Frederick Warne & Co., Ltd., 1933.

In addition to the above, there are many good reference books for the watercolorist, such as those on color by Cutler and Pepper, Denman Ross and Munsell; books on dynamic symmetry and other theories of composition; books on architectural perspective, and volumes of criticism of painting.